RUBBER
STAMPS

·RUBBER· STAMPS

AND HOW TO MAKE THEM

GEORGE L THOMSON

PANTHEON BOOKS
NEW YORK

Library of Congress Cataloging in Publication Data
Thomson, George Lawrie.
Rubber stamps and how to make them.
1. Rubber stamps. I. Title.
TS1920.T48   681'.6   82-6362
ISBN 0-394-71124-6   AACR2

Manufactured in the United States of America
First American Edition

CONTENTS

FOREWORD

A HISTORY OF STAMPS AND SEALS

Stamps or seals made in various materials have been used from the beginning of recorded history. The signet rings worn by many people today, and the universally used common rubber endorsing stamp with its ink pad are direct descendants of the Royal Seals of Gilgamesh, Hammurabi and the Pharaohs of ancient Egypt.

They were made in all kinds of materials – stone, clay, ivory, wood, bone, precious gems and gold, silver and other metals. When all writing was in cuneiform script, impressed on damp clay, many seals were cylindrical in form. They were rolled on the plastic surface to make the impression. The clay was then allowed to harden in the sun. Would you believe, the letter written on the slab of clay was often enclosed in an envelope of clay, which was inscribed with the address and sealed with the sender's personal stamp. Circular stamps were also in use at the same period.

Babylonian cylinder seal, about 4000 BC

Up till very recently, there were very few people who could read or write, but the sender of a letter had to be able to prove it was authentic. So after dictating it to a scribe, it was stamped with the person's specially cut seal, as difficult to forge as a written signature.

Each seal was individual and different. Some would have writing only, but many people had a picture too, usually connected with their trade or occupation. From the very beginning, seals were used by merchants and professional people as well as kings and nobles.

It is fascinating to note that the 4,000 year old seal from Ebla has a picture in the centre surrounded by an inscription – exactly the same arrangement as many modern rubber stamps.

Seal from Ebla (Syria), about 3000 BC

There are many variations in the shape: almond, oval, square, rectangular or polygonal, but round seems to have been most popular, being a logical and convenient shape to make and handle.

The Chinese and Japanese have used seals for thousands of years and still do. In Korea it is the custom to give a newly married couple a pair of hand engraved name seals as a wedding present.

Though for thousands of years seals were stamped on the document, there came a time when it became convenient to stamp the seal on a piece of softened wax attached to the document in some way. Many ancient documents written on vellum still survive, which have perhaps dozens of seals attached by signatories of the treaty, agreement or petition, some of whom probably could not write. In many cases, it was accepted that a seal was more "official" and authoritative than a mere inked signature.

Sometimes the seal was stamped into a piece of lead, as in the Papal Bull – an edict of the Pope. Bull is from the Latin, bulla, "a leaden seal". Documents even today can be sealed with a blob of sealing wax, stamped while still soft with a signet ring. Sometimes a calligrapher may write out some splendid scroll for a city or organisation, which then appends its own official seal.

Ancient Egyptian gold signet ring

Roman seal stamped in lead, about 3 AD

Since the invention of the rubber stamp however, most stamps are now directly on the document. One immediately thinks of passports, rubber stamped every time they are used. In any city office, a whole boxful of stamps may be found – date stamps, receipt stamps, "paid", "approved" or "cancelled" stamps and so on.

Sadly though, the *quality* of the stamps of this past century has fallen far below the standards set thousands of years previously. Few of today's commercially produced rubber stamps will be collected and appreciated in the future for their aesthetic value.

But perhaps *yours* will be!

Tutankhamen's seal, Egypt, about 1000 BC

The Great Seal of Islay, Scotland, 9th century

Town seal of Elgin, Scotland, about 11th century
Pre-Columbian seal (clay), S. America, 1300

Japanese woodcut seal, 18th century

Heraldic seal, England, 1329

Ecclesiastical seal, 15th century

Great Seal of King David II of Scotland, 1360

Handle of seal, 1388
Handle of seal, 18th century

11

MATERIALS AND TOOLS
YOU WILL NEED

Most of these may already be available in your house.

Rubber erasers, any size you can get. Choose the stiffer kinds, and avoid any very soft and elastic ones.

Needles or stiff wire

A rubber stamp pad, if you can only get one, make it a red one, with black as a second choice

Sandpaper, rough and smooth

Dowelling, cylindrical rods of wood, obtainable in hardware or art-supply stores, ½'' to 1'' in diameter

Square or rectangular section wood in lengths, also obtainable in hardware or art-supply stores, in various sizes to suit your stamps

A small saw to cut the last two items into suitable lengths for handles

A pair of pliers

Glue in tubes or rubber cement

Paper tissues or soft cloth

Carborundum stone to sharpen needle or wire

Old wooden pen handles or thin pieces of dowel, approx. ¼''

Smooth paper for taking prints on

Tracing paper

4b pencil obtainable at art-supply stores

Dip or fountain pen

Small piece of plastic sponge for cleaning stamps after printing

AN EXTRA NOTE ABOUT
THE MATERIALS

For making rubber stamps, erasers with clean cut edges are better than those with rounded edges, which can waste up to $\frac{1}{8}''$ all round the flat printing surface. Rectangular erasers are more economical to use than those cut in wedge shapes. The more springy or elastic erasers will require more care and time on cutting than the stiffer erasers.

In Britain, I have used a number of different textured erasers. The easiest to use so far has been the "WEB pencil eraser" made in Korea. In U.S.A. the ones I have tried are "Live-Line soft pink," "Live-Line soft pliable" (green), "Eberhard Faber Pink Pearl", "Eberhard Faber RubKleen" (green), and "Pedigree soft pink" and "soft pliable". The best for our purposes was "Pink Pearl", though still a bit too pliable. Eberhard Faber is the biggest – $2\frac{1}{2}'' \times 1\frac{1}{2}''$.

Tools which are useful in cutting are the X-acto series, the stencil knife and X-acto Nos 11 and 16. The Pickett Art Knife is very similar to X-acto No 11, but more expensive.

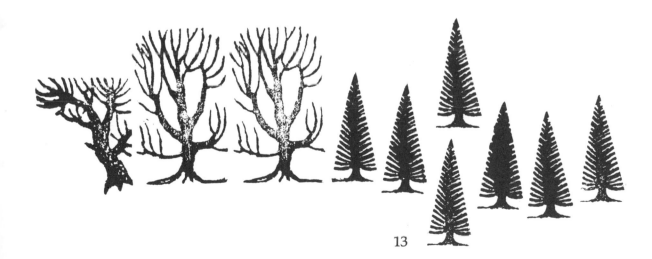

MAKING YOUR OWN STAMPS

Rubber in the form of rubber erasers or india rubbers is a universally available material; it comes in convenient sizes, is cheap compared with any other material, and most importantly, is the easiest to make clear prints from, using only hand pressure.

Owing to the elastic quality of rubber, it is not easy to make a controlled cut using a chisel, gouge or burin, or the usually recommended knife, which I myself used at the beginning.

Finally I devised a new method which works perfectly. No tools are specifically made for the purpose, so I made my own. You will also find it a simple matter to make your own tools, or adapt them from existing ones.

The two indispensables are, one fine needle point (1a), and one thick darning needle sharpened to a chisel point (1b) on a Carborundum stone. Simply push a half needle into a suitable piece of wood like an old wooden-handled pen with the nib-holding part cut off – *any* piece of wood the size and shape of a pencil.

Use a pair of flat-nosed pliers to hold the needle and push the point into the end of the handle for ½'' or so. Pull it out, cut it in half so as to leave about a 1'' length from the point.

Now with the pliers push the blunt end into the hole in the handle until only about ½'', or less, of the needle is showing. A springy or pliable needle should be pushed in until very little bending takes place when you are using it.

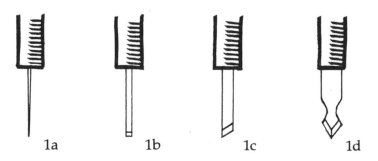

1a   1b   1c   1d

To get a reasonable width of chisel edge on your darning needle, cut it in half and dispose of the pointed end (or use it to make an extra tool!), then sharpen the cut end on the stone until it is like a tiny chisel.

Although these two tools you have made are capable of doing everything you need, you may like to add two more when you are proficient. These are, a very small scalpel (1c) and a stencil cutting nib (1d) as shown here. Even these can be made at home, but they are not at all essential.

To make your first rubber stamp, choose a suitable size of rubber eraser. Personally I like best to work with the white ones. Avoid any very soft or springy erasers. Work out a simple design on white paper and then, when you are satisfied it is as good as you can make it, take a soft HB pencil and draw it carefully onto tracing paper.

The design must of course be in REVERSE so that the imprint comes out the right way round – most important when using lettering.

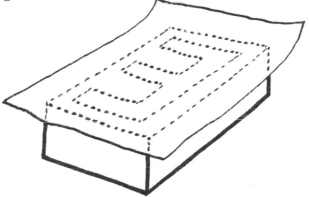

"But," you may be thinking, "I can't draw, I'm not an artist, I can't do letters, I can't make designs!" Don't despair! So long as you can get a piece of tracing paper, you can trace anything you fancy from books, magazines or papers. It can be a design, a letter or any small motif that appeals to you. No drawing skill is required. For your first trial rubber stamp, choose a broad and simple design. You can progress to more detailed work as you become more proficient.

15

Now, turn over the tracing paper, hold it firmly on the eraser so that it will not slip, and draw heavily over the lines of the design on the back which will transfer the drawing in reverse onto the eraser.

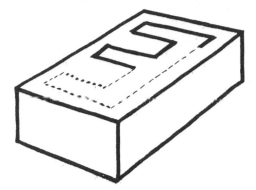

Re-draw with the soft pointed pencil, correcting any wobbly lines or missed parts. Draw over the lines carefully in ink to make them easier to see and to prevent them rubbing out while you're working. Use a pointed pen with black ink, with very little pressure. Never use ball-point pens which tend to dig into the eraser.

Hold the needle point tool like a pencil, and stroke very lightly along the outlines, towards yourself only – not backwards and forwards. Do this three or four times, deepening the cut to about one millimetre. Hold at a steep angle, sloping AWAY from the edge of the printing surface, not UNDER it. It is very important to keep to the OUTSIDE edge of the lines on your design. It is always possible to trim away surplus rubber, but there is no way to replace a piece cut away by accident. Do not try to score a long line at one go. It is better to use short strokes at first.

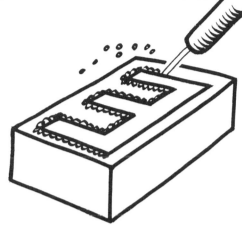

Continue picking out tiny crumbs with the chisel point (1b) until all the background has been removed. Do not make it any deeper than one millimetre at this stage. Note the slanted walls of the first cuts.

NEVER UNDERCUT. Undercutting will produce bad prints and these parts will eventually break off altogether. The printing surfaces must always have a good solid base, broad at the foot and narrowing at the top, like a railway embankment. Now with a moistened piece of tissue or soft cloth, carefully wipe off all the ink to prevent the dirtying of the printing ink. Dab the eraser on the ink pad until the printing surface is evenly covered and take your first print on a smooth piece of paper.

DON'T THUMP it as in stamping passports! Press firmly and don't wobble the stamp from side to side.

right

wrong

These prints show steps in the making of a stamp

There will be rough edges to be trimmed and high pieces of the background to be removed. Take care to keep the printing surface dead level or the design will print patchily.

Uneven edges may be scraped or "rubbed" away with the chisel edge held almost horizontal and at right angles to the line. This is also the best way to tidy curves.

From now on it is a patient process of gradually picking away all the bits of background high enough to print and tidying up edges, taking impressions as you go. I take an average of twenty prints before I am satisfied that the stamp is finished.

If there are large empty spaces inside your design, you will find the centre of the white space tends to pick up colour and print. You must dig away all the pieces of coloured background until it stays clear when printed. This is where the stiffer erasers score over the soft and very pliable ones, which need to be cleared much deeper, which leaves the printing surfaces less supported and liable to spread under pressure, making a smudgy print.

Leave the final tidying up until the background is quite clear. This makes it easier to spot roughness on the design itself. There are always one or two spots here and there to be taken out, or the occasional bulge where it shouldn't be on a line.

To make very fine white lines, hold the needle point vertically and stroke lightly along the line several times, not too deeply. About one millimetre is enough. If the line is too thin, thicken it by repeated stroking along the line, but make it no deeper.

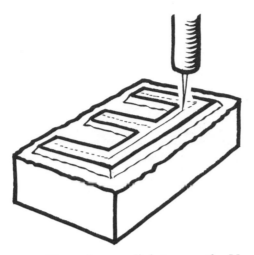

To make small dots, use the V-point held vertically and twirl with very light pressure until the dot is the right size. Dots *can* be made with the chisel edge, used the same way, but only one size.

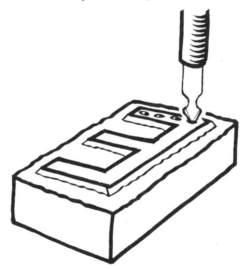

Small mistakes, when not too deep, may be corrected after rubbing down the surface smoothly again with a piece of fine sandpaper. Do not throw away the eraser if it cannot be repaired like this – use the other side or the edges if it is a thick one. If this too is spoiled, try rubbing down on a coarse sandpaper, finishing off with a smooth one. A large eraser, even if unevenly smoothed, can be cut into usable smaller pieces, and at the worst it can always be reverted to its original use!

I have one eraser with designs on all six faces, but I cannot recommend this. It's a nuisance when you want to use more than one of the designs, as you then have to sponge clean the one you have been using before you can go on, or put up with very inky fingers!

If you make a stamp you are really proud of and it gets accidentally damaged on the printing surface, you may be able to save it by rubbing it down slightly on fine sandpaper and re-trimming the bits which will inevitably thicken up. But before doing this, as a precaution take a print and, while it's still wet, press a new eraser on it to get an offset impression. From this you can cut an identical stamp. If you don't mind it being reversed, just print straight onto the new eraser *instead* of onto the paper first. This is how you can get a pair of angels for instance.

MAKING YOUR OWN HANDLES

To make handles, cut suitable lengths of round or square dowelling, or pieces of balsa wood and stick securely to the back of the seal. Balsa wood is light and easily worked with a sharp knife or razor blade, and sandpaper.

Most offices have out-of-date stamps, or damaged ones. If you can acquire some of these, you can peel off the old rubber and stick your own stamp on. As there are many different sizes, you may get one exactly the size you want.

For professional-looking handles, make friends with someone who has a lathe for turning wood!

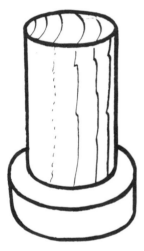
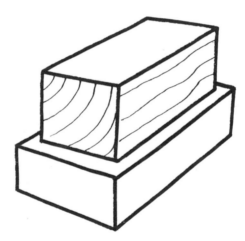

The seals should not overlap the handles more than ⅛" or so; but preferably they should not overlap at all. Try to get the seal and handle to match in size. A very small seal stuck on a very large mount is impossible to position when printing.

Some people prefer to put a layer of cellulose sponge between the stamp and the block of wood to which you are going to glue it. Many households use them for cleaning surfaces. The sponge can be up to ¼" thick. When you have cut your stamp, place it on the sponge and cut the sponge around it with a scalpel knife. Glue it onto the rubber stamp, then glue it onto your wood block.

Put some sort of mark on the stamp or the handle so that you know which way up to print. Handles are optional of course. The stamps print perfectly without one, though some people will find it difficult not to get inky fingers.

If you want your finished stamps to remain good-looking, put two or three coats of varnish on your wooden blocks – but remember – stamp your design on the block first, *then* varnish the block and finally glue it to the stamp.

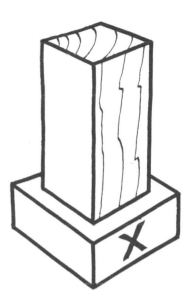

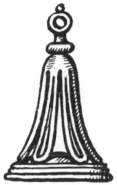

Robert Burns' seal, 1790

How long do stamps last? I read recently of someone who was still using stamps he cut as a schoolboy. And I know of commercially made rubber stamps from Victorian times which are still perfectly usable. I imagine you *could* wear them out by scrubbing with a toothbrush every time you clean them. I avoid any possibility of this by cleaning with a damp plastic sponge – the very fine ones are best. Dry with a soft cloth.

Remember to sponge off the colour you have been using before you start to use a different colour. The colour pads come in black, red, blue, green, violet and brown. They seem to last as long as the stamps, as long as you keep the lid shut, but you may need to add a drop of refreshing ink occasionally. This comes in conveniently small sized bottles.

24

LETTERS AND ENVELOPES

Your rubber stamps have many uses. They can be used as identification or purely as decoration on books, parcels, letters, envelopes – any smooth surface.

A stamp of your own house might make a good letter heading.

The white Cottage
Balgrie Bank, Bonnybank

Personalise your notepaper with your favourite flower or flowers.

Wednesday 14 September

Pepper Pike · OHIO · 44129

The Red Lion Guest House

 *Canterbury House*
Dartford
Chester · 1S43TL

You can design your own letter heading device, and if you make several motifs, change it at will.

26

Dear James
when are you going to visit our new house this
year? The garden is looking its best just

Dear Alice —

I have just received a note from the

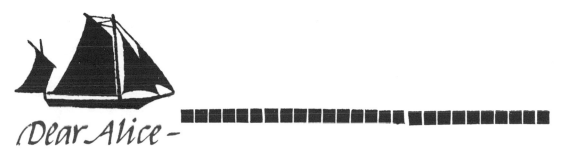

HAPPY EASTER • ANNA!

Suggestions for letter headings. Experiment with differ-
ent combinations of stamps and different colours.
Choose suitable stamps for the right occasion.
Use the same design on the envelope.

Stephanie Wolfe Murray.
Canongate Publishing.
17 Jeffrey Street. EH·1DR

Edinburgh

10p

1981

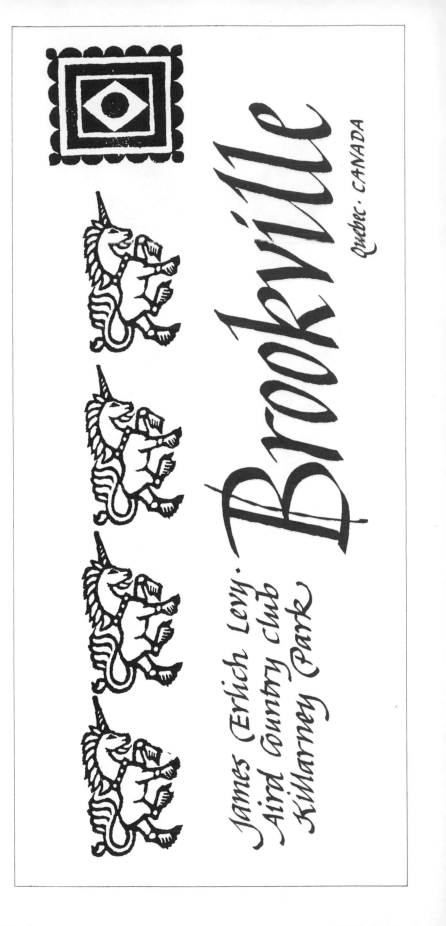

Brookville

Quebec · CANADA

James Erlich Levy · Aird Country Club · Killarney Park

Kenneth (B Eisenhauer · Art Publisher · Inc.

3206 Washington Avenue

(Boston

MASS.
03126

Elsie Gillespie · 11 Ephgrove Boulevard · PETERBOROUGH

Ontario CANADA

K9J 7E8

Harold Jefferson Eisenhower · Advertising Consultant · 3025 Carr Street

Ellenboro NSW Australia

Marianne Lindley · Southern Hospital
Shamba Road

Kitwe

Zambia

The appearance of letters and envelopes can be greatly enhanced by the use of suitable stamps.

Frame or mount for a postage stamp

Use your initials as a seal.

G.J.   B.B.   E.T.

Letters superimposed and reversed

The G.L. and T are superimposed and reversed to make an abstract pattern.

E. T. upsidedown now looks like a face. Use your stamps with imagination.

ABCDE
FGHIJK
LMNOP
QRSTU
VWXYZ

When you start your first alphabet set, this is the sort of lettering you should look for, with no fine lines or serifs to cause trouble in cutting.

Do not mix capitals of one type with small letters of another type. Be sure they belong together.

If you mount the stamps so that all the letter bases are flush with the edge of the mount (handle), you can then use a straight edge, as above, to place your letters against, thereby ensuring a straight line of lettering.

If you only have time or space for *one* alphabet, make this all capitals. Small letters can be added later if needed.

With a set of capital letters, small notices can be printed out in a short while. It is permissible to rule in guidelines with a soft pencil. The lines may be erased after the ink has dried.

The alphabet opposite is of *Versal* letters, which can be used as capitals or initials in handwritten letters.

Letters can be traced from newspapers and magazines, and a whole set of capitals and lower case letters may be built up. Some people write whole letters or even books this way – what patience!

SPRING
SALE

Even small place cards and posters are possible if you make an alphabet, or better still, make two – one of capital letters and one of small letters. Suitable letters to trace can be found in newspapers and magazines. Choose fairly simple, chunky letters; thin, spindly forms are unsuitable. If you do make an alphabet, start with a simple letter; I or L. Make the standard height one inch or thereabouts – most erasers have one dimension about this size.

E

Small stamps like these can be made if they contain only one or two words or signs.

Small signs like these can be useful.

Cut a complete alphabet and print your own posters, notices and broadsheets.

HAVE FUN!

YES!

SIMPLE BORDERS

Make short sections of simple borders, and print until
you have the length you want.

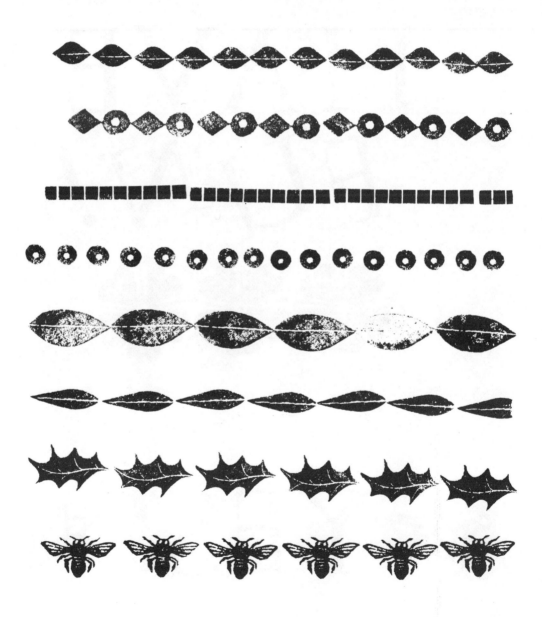

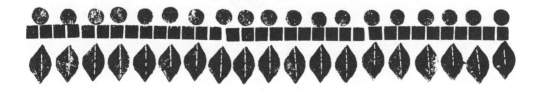

From a few basic elements, one can make simple frames
and cartouches, or more ambitiously, baroque borders,
as opposite.

44

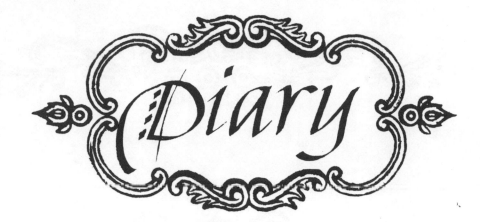

Titles like these can be printed directly on or inside books. Do a preliminary design on scrap paper so you know exactly what you are going to do on the book itself.

A great variety of labels can be made for all sorts of
purposes – wine, jam, herbs, books, address tags.

Some design elements for making cartouches and decoration

HISTORICAL AND HERALDIC SYMBOLS

Heraldry is a rich source of designs suitable for stamps. Look out for coats of arms and crests. Sometimes it is best just to use ONE part of a complicated design.

This galley is one element taken from the Arms of Clan Campbell. Thomsons are a *sept* of this clan.

A short-cut to a successful stamp is to look at ancient seals, and adapt the design for cutting in rubber. Usually the original artist has succeeded in simplifying his motif to make a small seal, and this simplification is just what you need in your stamp.

Based on the 12th century Great Seal of Islay, depicting Somerland and his three sons in their war galley after defeating the Viking fleet. Made for E. Gillespie, Ontario, Canada.

National or State symbols can often be improved by a fresh approach. Try looking at the animal, flower or whatever, in its original form, and re-design it in your own personal way.

Lion Rampant

Heraldic Lion

In Chinese philosophy and religion, the Yin and Yang symbol represents the two principles – one dark and feminine (Yin), the other light and masculine (Yang) – whose interaction influences our destinies. It is also a representation of good and evil. The spots mean there is a little bit of good in everything bad and a little bit of bad in everything good.

This is the *ankh*, the ancient Egyptian symbol meaning life.

Although this particular stamp is the badge of Clan Campbell – Wild Myrtle – the plant kingdom provides enough subjects for stamps to keep you busy for fifty years, and has been an inspiration to designers from the dawn of history.

Wild Myrtle: badge of Clan Campbell

Scots Thistle, designed from the actual plant. It is always wise to go to nature for information, rather than copy a copy of a copy of a copy!

Luckenbooth charms in the form of silver brooches, were made only in the Luckenbooths* in the High Street of Edinburgh (now the Royal Mile) in the 18th century. Small objects like brooches and coins can easily be translated into rubber stamps.

* *Lucken* means locking. A Luckenbooth was a permanent lock-up market stall.

These designs are based on decorations in the Book of Kells. Interlacings are a part of Celtic art, and in these animals I have tried to preserve some of this, even though there had to be considerable simplification. The originals are multi-coloured; try adding your own with coloured pens.

Celtic cross

This is based on an ancient Scottish silver brooch with a Celtic interlacing or knot pattern, simplified to cut in rubber.

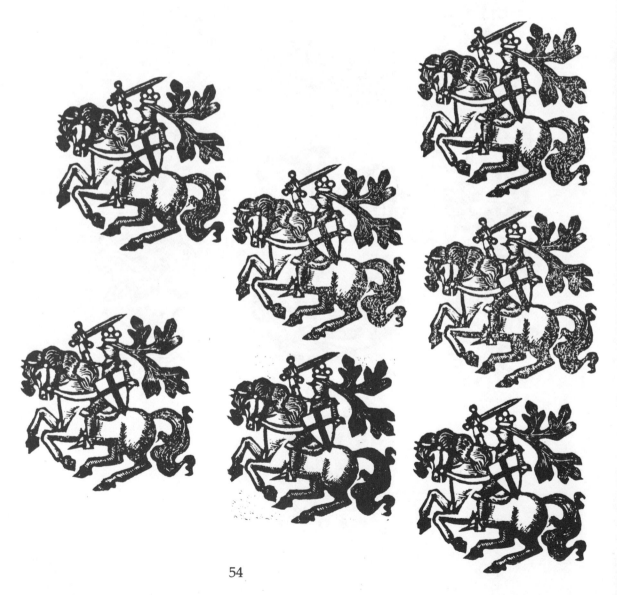

Egyptian friezes

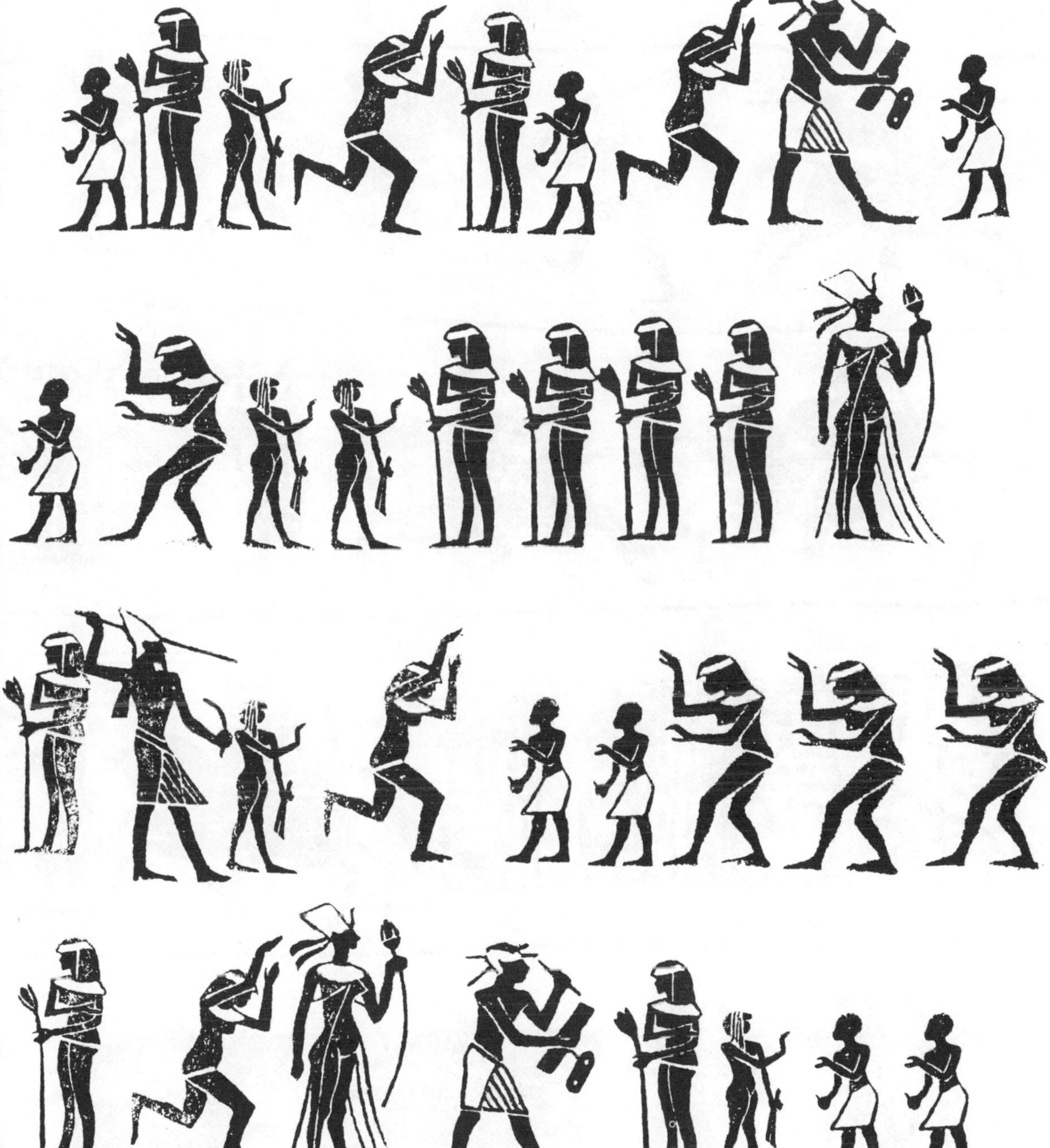

Bayeux tapestry

58

CHINESE SYMBOLS

HARMONY/UNDERSTANDING

These pages show a series of rubber stamps illustrating various ways of treating the design. If white on a coloured background, as above, it is *Yin*, or female. If coloured on a white background, it is *Yang*, or male. Chinese signs can be simplified, as here, or rendered like the original brush strokes, as in *Tiger*. They can be made any size, up to the largest eraser available. Those shown are not standardised in sets.

Tiger

Good Luck

Why

Nut

Pleased

"Small Dragon". A pictorial version

Happiness: this sign is always printed twice

Love

Peace

Blooming

Book

Certainly/surely

Mountain-man
A stamp made by Professor M. Rigg, Florida.

End

Though I have only worked on Chinese and Japanese characters, there is no reason whatsoever why we should not use any other source we can find. Avenues to be fruitfully explored are Eskimo, South American, African and Indian art – art from every race, in fact. American Indian designs are worth looking at; Bushman and Australian aboriginal designs would translate perfectly into this particular medium.

SIGNS OF THE CHINESE ZODIAC

Here are the twelve signs of the Chinese zodiac, which repeats every twelve years. To find which sign you were born under, add or subtract multiples of twelve from the date given with the sign.

Rat 1960

Ox 1961

Tiger 1962

Rabbit 1963

Dragon 1964

Snake 1965

Horse 1966

Sheep 1967

Monkey 1968

Cock 1969

Dog 1970

Boar 1971

Remember, the sign *means* the same even if the shape, size or proportions of the stamp are changed.

Year (see below, "Year of the Horse")

SIGNS OF THE WESTERN ZODIAC

Here are the signs of the Western zodiac, which covers
only one year, unlike the Chinese cycle of twelve years.

Aquarius

Pisces

Aries

Taurus

Gemini

Cancer

Leo

Virgo

Libra

Scorpio

Sagittarius

Capricorn

Designs may be naturalistic or formalised. If you design
a whole set, stick to *one* convention or style, and keep the
size of the designs equal.

ANIMALS

Animals are usually more effective when drawn in simple profile, with as few details as possible added.

64

Scottish hill farm.

Use your animals to make different pictures.

Animals of all kinds can be traced from photographs if you have no talent for drawing, but avoid involved perspective views. Mostly it is more effective to take a side view.

A stamp by Beki Blue, Sacramento, California. This is one stamp repeated three times and of course can be varied according to your taste. You could print a whole school of dolphins.

With mythical beasts, no one can accuse you of having got the details wrong!

CHRISTMAS/FESTIVALS

A variety of Christmas, Easter and other greetings stamps can be made.

For Christmas stamps, you have a choice of well-known symbols – the baby, the star, the three wise men and many others. You have to try not to put too much in the space you have at your disposal. Of course, other religions also have their own festivals, and these can supply just as many ideas worth making into stamps.

Draw circles with dividing lines first, as a guide when
making this snowflake.

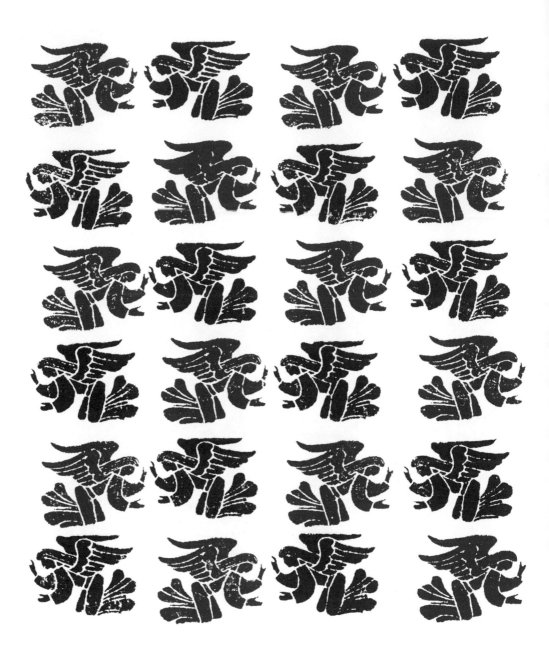

Special designs can be made for special occasions where wrapping paper is used – Christmas, birthdays, christenings and weddings. Use ordinary plain wrapping paper. Most will take a perfectly good print.

Make one or two different sizes of holly leaf for instant
Christmas decorations.

This stamp will appeal to vampires.

This is only one of the symbols connected with Halloween. Make a set for yourself – witches, moons, bogeys, pumpkin or turnip lanterns and so on.

HAVING FUN WITH YOUR STAMPS

On the following pages I will show you many examples of rubber stamps and what you can do with them. This may help you to get completely original ideas of your own.

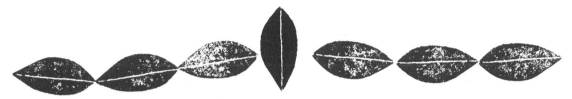

The very simplest leaf shape can be built up into attractive patterns. Try different sizes and shapes. Ink in lines to make stalks, not too straight.

75

Experiment with added leaves.

Bring your picture to life with insects.   Add a butterfly.

A dragonfly made from leaf shapes and some simple use of your pen.

Leaves and flowers

Even a beginner could make these Chinese leaves. Once
you have your basic shape no extra cutting is needed.

Make some wrapping paper.

A parcel could be decorated with a series of parallel stripes.

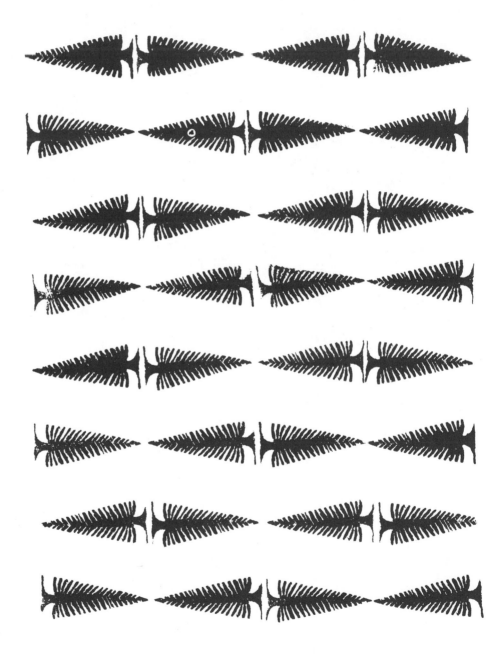

It is possible to make your own personalised gift wrapping paper or book coverings, by making an all-over repeat pattern, using perhaps several different colours.

On the following pages are ideas for wrapping paper for different occasions.

Two colour repeat design.

Stamps designed for one purpose can often be used in
other ways.

Turn your stamps sideways to get a different design.

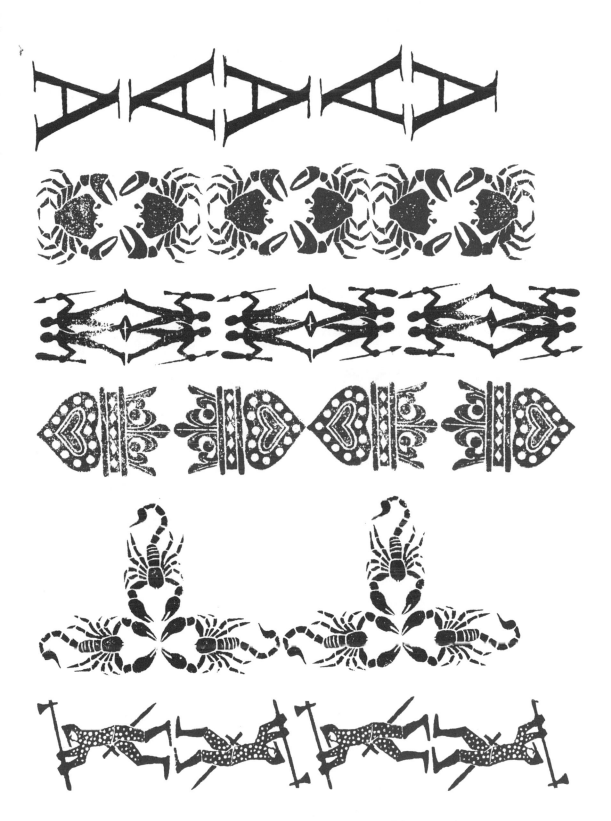

Sometimes people ask me to make a stamp for their company – here are a few examples.

1. Sensitive Plant (weaver)
2. Rowan, J. L. Hildry (agent)
3. John Ryder (typographer)
4. Malcolm Norden (miniature furniture)
5. Pamela J. Pavitt (embroiderer)
6/7. Pelican and Bayou Books (publishers)

1

2

3

hand made

malcolm
NORDEN

4

5

6

7

ABOUT THE AUTHOR

George Thomson was born in Scotland in 1916. He left school at fifteen having excelled in Art and English. There was no employment owing to the depression and no unemployment pay but he was fortunate to be given a scholarship to Edinburgh College of Art, at the exceptionally young age of sixteen.

George Thomson studied under Irene Wellington, possibly the finest calligrapher this century. She taught him the craft of calligraphy: using vellums, cutting quills, lettering and raised and flat gilding. It was an exceptionally broad course, covering drawing, painting, design and sculpture. He preferred this variety rather than the specialisation needed for a Diploma of Art, the necessary qualification for teaching. This decision caused him enormous problems later.

He was granted a post-diploma year and a travelling scholarship of £100. He immediately decided to cycle round the art centres of Europe which took seven months, covering France, Italy, Austria, Germany, Holland, Belgium and London. In all he covered 7,500 miles, leaving Austria the day before Hitler invaded the country.

George Thomson then worked in London in the Art Department of the *Radio Times,* returning to Edinburgh just before war broke out. He was called up and became an aircraft fitter, an engineering inspector and an illustrative draughtsman.

In 1945 he started a studio in Edinburgh, but it was too soon, no work. In 1947 he moved to Burntisland in Fife, living in a hut, where he grew his own food, most of which was eaten by animals, pests or stolen. In desperation he went to teach for a month at Kirkcaldy High School and discovered he loved it and was highly regarded by both staff and pupils. However, bureaucracy stepped in; he was not a qualified teacher. He went back to art school, took a teacher training course and had his first book *Better Handwriting* published by Penguin. It became an immediate best-seller. Finally, four years later, he returned to Kirkcaldy, this time as principal art teacher.

In 1967 George Thomson retired from teaching and started to work on his own again – something he had no time or energy to do as a teacher. He has had numerous commissions, not only for calligraphic work but also for wood and stone carving, pottery, book binding, engraving, to name but a few.

In the last few years George Thomson has been to Florida and California as a visiting lecturer where they are currently discovering the joys of using rubber stamps. It was about two years ago that he began to carve seals out of stone, wood and then rubber, a craft which is a curious combination of the skills he has acquired over the years. He has developed a method of making stamps that is utterly simple and effective. There is probably no finer craftsman today working in this medium.

If you'd like to make stamps as
presents for your friends, but
can't find the time —
then write for information to the
addresses below. All the designs
in this book and many more are
available in hand-crafted duplicate.
Complete sets of related subjects and
alphabets can be made up to order.

B · M · BLUE
(P · O · Box 60925 [D · G]
Sacramento · CALIFORNIA · 95841 · U·S·A
in U·K —
White Cottage · Balgriebank · LEVEN · KY85SL

s·a·e please !